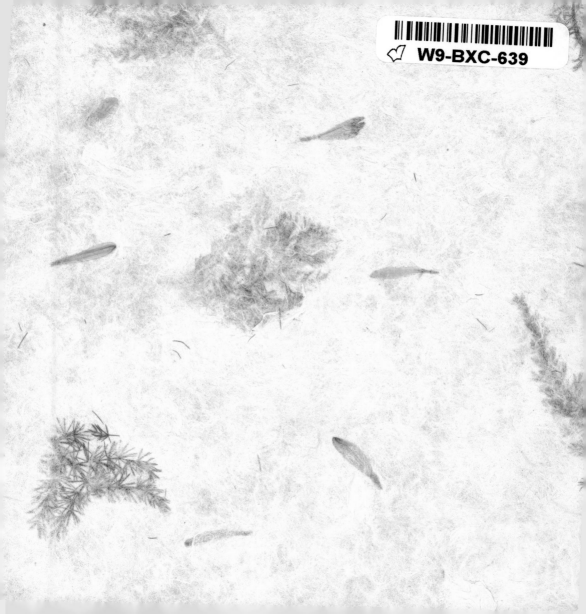

————————————————

*P*ositive thinking... is the key
which unlocks the doors of
the world.

Samuel McChord Crothers

Other books in the *"Language of" Series...* by

Blue Mountain Press ®

The Language of Love

The Language of Friendship

The Language of Happiness

The Language of Marriage

The Language of Success

The Language of Teaching

The Language of Courage and Inner Strength

Thoughts to Share with a Wonderful Mother

Thoughts to Share with a Wonderful Father

Thoughts to Share with a Wonderful Son

Thoughts to Share with a Wonderful Daughter

It's Great to Have a Brother like You

It's Great to Have a Sister like You

The Language of

POSITIVE
THINKING

A Collection from Blue Mountain Arts®

Blue Mountain Press®

Boulder, Colorado

ACKNOWLEDGMENTS appear on page 48.

Library of Congress Catalog Card Number: 99-047783
ISBN: 0-88396-541-0

Manufactured in Thailand
First Printing: September 1999

 This book is printed on recycled paper.

Library of Congress Cataloging-in-Publication Data

The language of positive thinking : a collection from Blue Mountain Arts.

    p.   cm.

  ISBN 0-88396-541-0 (alk. paper)

   1. Self-actualization (Psychology)--Quotations, maxims, etc. 2. Optimism--Quotations, maxims, etc. 3. Motivation (Psychology)--Quotations, maxims, I. Title: Positive thinking.
II. Blue Mountain Arts (Firm).

  BF637.S4.B575 1999

  158.1--dc21

99-047783
CIP

Blue Mountain Press INC.

P.O. Box 4549, Boulder, Colorado 80306

# Contents

(Authors listed in order of first appearance)

Have Positive Thoughts, and Always "Hang in There"

Difficulties arise in the lives of us all. What is most important is dealing with the hard times, coping with the changes, and getting through to the other side where the sun is still shining just for you.

It takes a strong person to deal with tough times and difficult choices. But you are a strong person. It takes courage. But you possess the inner courage to see you through. It takes being an active participant in your life. But you are in the driver's seat, and you can determine the direction you want tomorrow to go in.

Hang in there... and take care to see that you don't lose sight of the one thing that is constant, beautiful, and true: Everything will be fine — and it will turn out that way because of the special kind of person you are.

So... beginning today and lasting a lifetime through — hang in there, and don't be afraid to feel like the morning sun is shining... just for you.

— Collin McCarty

There is nothing either good or bad,
but thinking makes it so.

 William Shakespeare

The happiness habit is developed by simply practicing happy thinking. Make a mental list of happy thoughts and pass them through your mind several times every day. If an unhappiness thought should enter your mind, immediately stop, consciously eject it, and substitute a happiness thought. Every morning before arising, lie relaxed in bed and deliberately drop happy thoughts into your conscious mind. Let a series of pictures pass across your mind of each happy experience you expect to have during the day. Savor their joy. Such thoughts will help cause events to turn out that way.

Norman Vincent Peale

Positive Thinkers Have
Twelve Qualities in Common

They have confidence in themselves
They have a very strong sense of purpose
They never have excuses for not doing something
They always try their hardest for perfection
They never consider the idea of failing
They work extremely hard towards their goals
They know who they are
They understand their weaknesses as well as their
    strong points
They can accept and benefit from criticism
They know when to defend what they are doing
They are creative
They are not afraid to be a little different in
    finding innovative solutions that will enable
        them to achieve their dreams

 Susan Polis Schutz

Whatever Else You Do

Whatever else you do or forbear,
impose upon yourself the task of happiness;
and now and then abandon yourself
to the joy of laughter.

And however much you condemn
the evil in the world, remember that the
world is not all evil; that somewhere
children are at play, as you yourself in the
old days; that women still find joy
in the stalwart hearts of men;

And that men, treading with restless feet
their many paths, may yet find refuge
from the storms of the world in the cheerful
house of love.

Max Ehrmann

"Out of every earth day,
make a little bit of heaven."

There is nothing which can hinder or circumvent a strong and determined soul seeking for health, usefulness, truth and success.

Keep that fact well in mind and live to it, no matter what the whole world may say to the contrary. Fear nothing. You are a part of the splendid universe, and you are here to get the best out of this phase of life…. Look for something to be thankful and glad over each day, and you will find it….

Fill your soul and mind full of love
and sympathy and joy…
and blessings
will follow.

 Ella Wheeler Wilcox

Make Each Day a New Beginning

Finish every day and be done with it. You have done what you could. Some blunders and absurdities no doubt crept in; forget them as soon as you can. Tomorrow is a new day; begin it well and serenely and with too high a spirit to be cumbered with your old nonsense. This day is all that is good and fair. It is too dear, with its hopes and invitations, to waste a moment on the yesterdays.

 Ralph Waldo Emerson

Look not mournfully into the Past. It comes not back again. Wisely improve the Present. It is thine. Go forth to meet the shadowy Future, without fear, and with a manly heart.

 Henry Wadsworth Longfellow

Do what you can, with what you have, where you are.

 Theodore Roosevelt

Start Where You Stand

Start where you stand and never mind the past,
  The past won't help you in beginning new,
If you have left it all behind at last
    Why, that's enough, you're done with it, you're
      through;
This is another chapter in the book,
  This is another race that you have planned,
Don't give the vanished days a backward look,
  Start where you stand.

The world won't care about your old defeats
  If you can start anew and win success,
The future is your time, and time is fleet
    And there is much of work and strain and stress;
Forget the buried woes and dead despairs,
  Here is a brand new trial right at hand,
The future is for him who does and dares,
  Start where you stand.

Old failures will not halt, old triumphs aid,
  To-day's the thing, to-morrow soon will be;
Get in the fight and face it unafraid,
    And leave the past to ancient history;
What has been, has been; yesterday is dead
    And by it you are neither blessed nor banned,
Take courage, man, be brave and drive ahead,
  Start where you stand.

Berton Braley

Difficult Times
Don't Last Forever

Sometimes, the problems
you must face
are more than you wish
to cope with,
and tomorrow doesn't seem
to offer any solutions.

You may ask yourself "Why me?"
but the answer is sometimes unclear.
You may even tend to feel
that life hasn't been just or fair
to burden you with such obstacles.

The roads any of us choose
to follow are never free
of bumps or curves,
but eventually the turns
lead to a smoother path ahead.

Believe in yourself and your dreams.
You will soon realize that
the future holds many promises
for you.
Remember... difficult times
don't last forever.

 — Geri Danks

Enthusiasm and Optimism Can Overcome Any Obstacle

The greater the difficulty, the greater the glory.

Cicero

Enthusiasm is one of the most powerful engines of success. When you do a thing, do it with all your might.... Be active, be energetic, be enthusiastic and faithful, and you will accomplish your objective.

Ralph Waldo Emerson

Optimism is the faith that leads to achievement; nothing can be done without hope.

 Helen Keller

Climb

Go higher than you ever thought you could. Climb the ladder of success, whatever that is for you. Climb your way to the top. Take as long as you need: no one is watching the clock (except maybe you). Before you reach out to hold onto something or somebody, make certain it's strong enough to support you. Grit your teeth and scrape your knees and bleed and sweat. If your mountain is simply to get through the day, then scale it. When you get to the top, look back at what you've accomplished. Now smile or holler or cry. Before you head for the valley and the *next* mountain, remember the women who have gone before you and the ones who will follow your climb.

 Rachel Snyder

❧ Transform Failure into Success! ❧

You must accept that you might fail; then, if you do your best and still don't win, at least you can be satisfied that you've tried. If you don't accept failure as a possibility, you don't set high goals, you don't branch out, you don't try — you don't take the risk.

 Rosalynn Carter

A man should never be ashamed to say he has been in the wrong, which is but saying in other words that he is wiser today than he was yesterday.

 Alexander Pope

Little minds are tamed and subdued by misfortune, but great minds rise above it.

 Washington Irving

Probably he who never made a mistake
never made a discovery.

Samuel Smiles

The glory is not in never failing,
but in rising every time you fail.

Chinese Proverb

I am not discouraged, because every wrong
attempt discarded is another step forward.

Thomas A. Edison

We learn wisdom from failure
much more than from success.

Samuel Smiles

The men who try to do something and fail
are infinitely better than those who try to do
nothing and succeed.

Lloyd Jones

You *have* choice. You can select joy over despair. You can select happiness over tears. You can select action over apathy. You can select growth over stagnation. You can select you. And you can select life. And it's time that people tell you you're not at the mercy of forces greater than yourself. You are, indeed, the *greatest* force for *you*.

 Leo Buscaglia

You owe no one as much as you owe yourself. You owe to yourself the action that opens for you the doors to the goodness, the variety, and the excitement of effort and success, of battle and victory. Making payment on this debt to yourself is the exact opposite of selfishness. You can best pay your debt to society, that has made you what you are, by being just yourself with all your might and as a matter of course.... You fulfill the promise that lies latent within you by keeping your promises to yourself.

David Harold Fink

Attitude Is Everything

The longer I live, the more I realize the impact of attitude on life. It is more important than the past, than education, than money, than circumstances, than failures, than successes, than what other people think or say or do. It is more important than appearance, giftedness or skill. It will make or break a company... a church... a home. The remarkable thing is we have a choice every day regarding the attitude we will embrace for that day. We cannot change our past... we cannot change the fact that people will act in a certain way. We cannot change the inevitable. The only thing we can do is play on the one string we have, and that is our attitude.... I am convinced that life is 10% what happens to me and 90% how I react to it. And so it is with you... we are in charge of our Attitudes.

 Anonymous

Positive Thinking Is...

...like gasoline: A whole tankful won't do much good until we put our foot on the gas pedal and start driving. Positive thinking makes action possible: Action brings our good thoughts to life. Positive thinking, positive action.

Arnold Fox, M.D. and Barry Fox, Ph.D.

...the key which unlocks the doors of the world. There is something in us which corresponds to that which is around us, beneath us, and above us.

Samuel McChord Crothers

...not always the easiest course of action when confronting difficulties. If, however, we can remain focused on keeping hope strong and not succumbing to negative influences, we will meet with success in dealing with anything life may throw in our path.

Hiram Rogers Lloyd

...a habit, like any other; we can practice it every day until it becomes second nature to us — and along the way, transform our lives.

Washington L. Crowley

...knowing that, in the grand scheme of things, we live in a world where rainy days eventually give way to sunnier skies.

R. L. Keith

...a constant attention to the details that make up an average day — with the knowledge that how you live this moment may reflect on the rest of your life.

 Jason Rogerson

...the ultimate triumph of mind over matter; the victory of the spirit over all the shadows lurking in the world.

 Martin A. Browning

...the most effective tool ever created for lifting an individual to the greatest achievements humanity can aspire to.

 Montague Edwards

❖ Positive Thinking Is... ❖

Joy
> in your heart,
> your mind,
> your soul.

Peace
> with yourself
> and with the universe.

Harmony.

Courage
> to feel,
> to need,
> to reach out.

Freedom
> to let yourself
> be bound by love.

Friendship.
Wisdom
      to learn,
      to change,
      to let go.
Acceptance
      of the truth
      and beauty within yourself.
Growth.
Pleasure
      in all that you see,
      and touch,
      and do.
Happiness
      with yourself
      and with the world.
Love.

Maureen Doan

Look on the Bright Side

For every negative that consumes your happiness,
Affirm two positives that sustain you.

For every "should've" you wish you'd done,
Acknowledge something you're glad you did.

For every loss that has altered your world,
Count from it something you have gained.

For every limit that has ever beset you,
Consider your possibilities.

You can't always change the way things are,
But you can change the way you wish to see them.
Never stop looking
For the brighter side and beyond.

Eric T. Moore

When I think of my past,
I try to dwell on the good times,
the happy moments, and not to be
                haunted by the bad...
To me the gift of life is
contained in the command,
whatever happens: "Don't let it get you.
                Just keep on going."
Thus... I try to think
of the good that I have
already experienced
and what will
still be coming.

Rose Kennedy

To Be Free

In each of us there is an urge to be free. To live life without worry and stress and distress and pain.

We all want to be free from,

Frustration,
    Guilt,
        Resentment,
           Blame
             Fear
               Anger
                    Discouragement
                Worry
and freedom from unfulfilled desires.

                            To be really free you must unlock the gate that holds your higher self imprisoned in darkness and anguish.

The key to this gate lies deep within your being. It is hidden behind years of disappointment and unexpressed desires.
To find it you will have to look with courage and calm.

You must persist when you feel that the search is in vain. For to be truly free the search must begin and once begun you cannot go back.

And it is not a search for timid souls.

The road inside is cluttered with all sorts of baggage and illusions as well as erroneous beliefs that have become etched on your mind.

Your key to freedom lies in your power to control your thoughts.

 Tim Connor

Maintaining Optimism
Is a Lifelong Process

Positive thinking is not the destination; it is the journey. An optimistic person will be constantly challenged — by external circumstances as well as inner fears and doubts. Always remember that these tests are like a ladder you must climb.

As you move past each rung, your optimism strengthens and your confidence begins to flex newly found muscle that you might never have developed otherwise.

— Montague Edwards

Always think on the bright side —
 no matter what life brings
  to your day.
You'll gain a treasure within your soul
 that no worry or hardship
  can ever take away.

 Isaac Purcell

We do a lot of vacillating between old ideas and new ways of thinking. Be patient with yourself through this process. Beating yourself up only keeps you stuck. It's better to build yourself up instead. Anything you say or think is an affirmation. Really be aware of your thoughts and your words; you might discover that a lot of them are very negative. Many people tend to approach life through negative eyes. They take an ordinary situation like a rainy day and say something like, "Oh what a terrible day." It isn't a terrible day. It's a wet day. To create a wonderful day sometimes takes just a slight change in the way you look at it. Be willing to let go of an old, negative way that you look at something, and look at it in a new, positive way.

 Louise L. Hay

Thinking as a
One-Hundred-Percent-of-the-Time
Winner

Thinking like a winner means not always having to defeat someone else. It means being able to grow from a situation in which you fail to reach your goal. It involves not demanding perfection from yourself in every single thing you do, but, instead, thinking of yourself as perfect and thus capable of growing. It means reminding yourself that perfection doesn't mean staying the same; it means being able to allow yourself to grow. Thinking as a winner means not coming down on yourself; it means refusing to allow self-repudiating thoughts into your head. It involves pushing out the inclination to evaluate yourself in comparison with others, and giving yourself permission to be the unique person you are.

Dr. Wayne W. Dyer

We never have more than we can bear. The present hour we are always able to endure. As is our day, so is our strength. If the trials of many years were gathered into one, they would overwhelm us... but all is so wisely measured to our strength that the bruised reed is never broken.

 H. E. Manning

I am not bound to win, but I am bound to be true. I am not bound to succeed, but I am bound to live up to the light I have.

Abraham Lincoln

Ten Thoughts to Help You
Avoid Discouragement

1. Look at life as a journey and enjoy the ride. Get the most out of the detours and realize they're sometimes necessary.

2. Do your best, but if what you've been doing has caused you discouragement, try a different approach. Be passionate about the process, but don't be so attached to the outcome.

3. Wish the best for everyone, with no personal strings attached. Applaud someone else's win as much as you would your own.

4. Trust that there's a divine plan, that we don't always know what's best for us. A disappointment now could mean a victory later, so don't be disappointed. There is usually a reason.

5. Ask no more of yourself than the best that you can do, and be satisfied with that. Be compassionate toward yourself as well as others. Know your calling, your gift, and do it well.

6. Don't worry about something after it's done; it's out of your hands then, too late, over! Learn the lesson and move on.

7. Have the attitude that no one, except you, owes you anything. Give without expecting a thank-you in return. But when someone does something for you, be appreciative of even the smallest gesture.

8. Choose your thoughts or your thoughts will choose you; they will free you or keep you bound. Educate your spirit and give it authority over your feelings.

9. Judge no one, and disappointment and forgiveness won't be an issue. No one can let you down if you're not leaning on them. People can't hurt you unless you allow them to.

10. Love anyway... for no reason... and give... just because.

 Donna Fargo

Within You Is the Power...

If you are distressed by anything external, the pain is not due to the thing itself but to your own estimate of it; and this you have the power to revoke at any moment.

 Marcus Aurelius

No man is free who is not master of himself.

 Epictetus

In the depth of winter, I finally learned that within me there lay an invincible summer.

 Albert Camus

The only conquests which are permanent, and leave no regrets, are our conquests over ourselves.

 Napoleon Bonaparte

Invictus

Out of the night that covers me,
　　Black as the Pit from pole to pole,
I thank whatever gods may be
　　For my unconquerable soul.

In the fell clutch of circumstance
　　I have not winced nor cried aloud.
Under the bludgeonings of chance
　　My head is bloody, but unbowed.

Beyond this place of wrath and tears
　　Looms but the Horror of the shade,
And yet the menace of the years
　　Finds, and shall find, me unafraid.

It matters not how strait the gate,
　　How charged with punishments the scroll,
I am the master of my fate:
　　I am the captain of my soul.

 William Ernest Henley

# Always Have Hope

Hope is the thing with feathers —
That perches in the soul —
And sings the tune without the words —
And never stops — at all —

— Emily Dickinson

Hope is the better half of courage.
Hope! has it not sustained the work,
and given the fainting heart time and
patience to outwit the chances and
changes of life.

Honoré de Balzac

Hope is like the sun which, as we journey
towards it, casts the shadow of our burden
behind us.

 Samuel Smiles

Hope

Hope is not the closing of your eyes
to the difficulty, the risk,
or the failure.

It is a trust that —
if I fail now —
I shall not fail forever;
and if I am hurt,
I shall be healed.

It is a trust that
life is good,
love is powerful,
and the future is full of promise.

 Anonymous

If we will do the following five things, we will have the strength to be strong in hard moments, in testing times.

- Never make a promise we will not keep.
- Make meaningful promises, resolutions, and commitments to do better and to be better — and share these with a loved one.
- Use self-knowledge and be very selective about the promises we make.
- Consider promises as a measure of our integrity and faith in ourselves.
- Remember that our personal integrity or self-mastery is the basis for our success with others.

Stephen R. Covey

See It Through

When you're up against a trouble,
    Meet it squarely, face to face;
Lift your chin and set your shoulders,
    Plant your feet and take a brace.
When it's vain to try to dodge it,
    Do the best that you can do;
You may fail, but you may conquer,
    See it through!

Black may be the clouds about you
    And your future may seem grim,
But don't let your nerve desert you;
    Keep yourself in fighting trim.
If the worse is bound to happen,
    Spite of all that you can do,
Running from it will not save you,
    See it through!

Even hope may seem but futile,
    When with troubles you're beset,
But remember you are facing
    Just what other men have met.
You may fail, but fall still fighting;
    Don't give up, whate'er you do;
Eyes front, head high to the finish.
    See it through!

Edgar A. Guest

This, Too, Shall Pass Away

When some great sorrow, like a mighty river,
   Flows through your life with peace-destroying power,
And dearest things are swept from sight forever,
   Say to your heart each trying hour:
      "This, too, shall pass away."

When ceaseless toil has hushed your song of gladness,
   And you have grown almost too tired to pray,
Let this truth banish from your heart its sadness,
   And ease the burdens of each trying day:
      "This, too, shall pass away."

When fortune smiles, and, full of mirth and pleasure,
 The days are flitting by without a care,
Lest you should rest with only earthly treasure,
 Let these few words their fullest import bear:
  "This, too, shall pass away."

When earnest labor brings you fame and glory,
 And all earth's noblest ones upon you smile,
Remember that life's longest, grandest story
 Fills but a moment in earth's little while:
  "This, too, shall pass away."

 Ella Wheeler Wilcox

Happiness in this world, when it comes, comes incidentally. Make it the object of pursuit, and it leads us on a wild-goose chase, and is never attained. Follow some other object, and very possibly we may find that we have caught happiness without dreaming of it.

 Nathaniel Hawthorne

Happiness cannot come from without. It must come from within. It is not what we see and touch or that which others do for us which makes us happy; it is that which we think and feel and do, first for the other fellow and then for ourselves.

Helen Keller

Find Happiness
in Everything You Do

Find happiness in nature
in the beauty of a mountain
in the serenity of the sea
Find happiness in friendship
in the fun of doing things together
in the sharing and understanding
Find happiness in your family
in the stability of knowing
        that someone cares
in the strength of love and honesty
Find happiness in yourself
in your mind and body
in your values and achievements
Find happiness in
everything
you
do

 Susan Polis Schutz

Be a Positive Thinker, and Don't Ever Give Up!

Remember… there is a deeper strength
and an amazing abundance of peace
available to you.
Draw from this well;
call on your faith to uphold you.
You will make it through this time
and find joy in life again.

Life continues around us,
even when our troubles seem to stop time.
There is good in life every day.
Take a few minutes to distract yourself
from your concerns —
long enough to draw strength from a tree
or to find pleasure in a bird's song.

Return a smile;
realize that life is a series of levels,
cycles of ups and downs —
some easy, some challenging.
Through it all, we learn;
we grow strong in faith;
we mature in understanding.
The difficult times are often
the best teachers, and there is
good to be found in all situations.
Reach for the good.
Be strong, and don't give up.

 Pamela Owens Renfro

ACKNOWLEDGMENTS

We gratefully acknowledge the permission granted by the following authors, publishers, and authors' representatives to reprint poems or excerpts from their publications.

Simon & Schuster for "The happiness habit is developed by..." from THE POWER OF POSITIVE THINKING by Norman Vincent Peale, published by Ballantine Books, a division of Random House, Inc. Copyright © 1952, 1956 by Prentice-Hall, Inc., copyrights renewed 1980, 1984 by Norman Vincent Peale. All rights reserved. Reprinted by permission.

Robert L. Bell for "Whatever Else You Do" by Max Ehrmann. Copyright © 1948 by Bertha K. Ehrmann. All rights reserved. Reprinted by permission of Robert L. Bell, Melrose, MA 02176, USA.

NTC/Contemporary Publishing Group, Inc. for "Climb" from 365 WORDS OF WELL-BEING FOR WOMEN by Rachel Snyder, published by Contemporary Books, an imprint of NTC/Contemporary Publishing Company. Copyright © 1997 by Rachel Snyder. All rights reserved. Reprinted by permission.

The University of Arkansas Press for "You must accept that you might fail..." from EVERYTHING TO GAIN by Jimmy and Rosalynn Carter. Copyright © 1987, 1995 by Jimmy and Rosalynn Carter. All rights reserved. Reprinted by permission.

The Leo F. Buscaglia Trust for "You have choice" from LIVING, LOVING & LEARNING by Leo Buscaglia, Ph.D., published by Ballantine Books, a division of Random House, Inc. Copyright © 1982 by Leo F. Buscaglia, Inc. All rights reserved. Reprinted by permission.

Hay House, Inc. for "Positive thinking is... like gasoline..." from BEYOND POSITIVE THINKING: PUTTING YOUR THOUGHTS INTO ACTION by Arnold Fox, M.D. and Barry Fox, Ph.D. Copyright © 1991 by Arnold Fox, M.D. and Barry Fox, Ph.D. All rights reserved. Reprinted by permission. And for "We do a lot of vacillating between old ideas..." from MEDITATIONS TO HEAL YOUR LIFE by Louise L. Hay. Copyright © 1994 by Louise L. Hay. All rights reserved. Reprinted by permission.

Eric T. Moore for "Look on the Bright Side." Copyright © 1999 by Eric T. Moore. All rights reserved. Reprinted by permission.

Doubleday, a division of Random House, Inc., for "When I think of my past..." from TIMES TO REMEMBER by Rose F. Kennedy. Copyright © 1974 by the Joseph P. Kennedy, Jr. Foundation. All rights reserved. Reprinted by permission.

Tim Connor for "To Be Free." Copyright © 1999 by Tim Connor. All rights reserved. Reprinted by permission.

Pocket Books, a division of Simon & Schuster, Inc., for "Thinking as a One-Hundred-Percent-of-the-Time-Winner" from THE SKY'S THE LIMIT by Dr. Wayne W. Dyer. Copyright © 1980 by Wayne W. Dyer. All rights reserved. Reprinted by permission.

PrimaDonna Entertainment Corp. for "Ten Thoughts to Help You Avoid Discouragement" by Donna Fargo. Copyright © 1999 by PrimaDonna Entertainment Corp. All rights reserved. Reprinted by permission.

Simon & Schuster, Inc. for "If we will do the following five things..." from PRINCIPLE-CENTERED LEADERSHIP by Stephen R. Covey, published by Summit Books. Copyright © 1990, 1991 by Stephen R. Covey. All rights reserved. Reprinted by permission.

A careful attempt has been made to trace the ownership of poems and excerpts used in this anthology in order to obtain permission to reprint copyrighted materials and give proper credit to the copyright owners. If any error or omission has occurred, it is completely inadvertent, and we would like to make corrections in future editions provided that written notification is made to the publisher:

BLUE MOUNTAIN PRESS, INC., P.O. Box 4549, Boulder, Colorado 80306